Bud the Pup

Illustrated by Karen Bell

High-Frequency Words					
a	the	was	he	said	with

Scott
Foresman

Editorial Offices: Glenview, Illinois • Parsippany, New Jersey • New York, New York
Sales Offices: Parsippany, New Jersey • Duluth, Georgia • Glenview, Illinois
Coppell, Texas • Ontario, California

Diz had a pet pup.

The pup was Bud.

He fed him.

Diz hid in a box with
Bud the pup.

Diz said, "Run, Bud."

He ran in the sun with
Bud the pup.

Mom said, "Diz? Bud?"

He was with Bud the pup.